P9-DBX-268

PHYSICS

Text and design copyright © Toucan Books Ltd. 2009
Based on an original copyright by Toucan Books Ltd.
Illustrations copyright © Simon Basher 2009
Published in the United States by Kingfisher
175 Fifth Avenue, New York, NY 10010.
Kingfisher is an imprint of Macmillan Children's Books, London.

Consultant: Dr. Mike Goldsmith
Editorial consultant: Giles Sparrow

Designed and created by Basher
www.basherbooks.com

Dedicated to Henry Theobalds

Distributed in the U.S. by Macmillan, 175 Fifth Ave., New York, NY 10010
Distributed in Canada by H. B. Fenn and Company Ltd., 34 Nixon Road, Bolton, Ontario L7E 1W2

Library of Congress Cataloging-in-Publication Data
Green, Dan.
Physics / Dan Green ; Simon Basher, illustrator.—1st ed.
p. cm.
Includes index.
ISBN 978-0-7534-6214-0
1. Physics—Juvenile literature. I. Basher, Simon, ill. II. Title.
QC25.G738 2008
530—dc22
2007031805

ISBN: 978-0-7534-6612-4

Kingfisher books are available for special promotions and premiums.
For details contact: Special Markets Department, Macmillan, 175 Fifth Avenue, New York, NY 10010

For more information, please visit www.kingfisherbooks.com

Printed in China
10 9 8 7 6 5 4 3 2 1
1TR/1010/WKT/SCHOY/140MA

CONTENTS

Physics

Introduction

- The study of energy and matter and how they interact
- The most fundamental and far reaching of all the sciences
- There's much more to the universe than meets the eye. . . .

Physics is all about knowing—or trying to find out—what makes the universe tick. It started out with some naturally nosy people who wanted to know why the things around them did what they did. Nothing has changed today, but over the past few hundred years, we've realized that there are whole worlds both bigger and smaller than our human senses can detect.

Physics can be daunting at first, full of facts and formulas, but this book peels back the stuffy layers to show you the main players behind the scenes. You'll meet everyday characters, such as Friction, who slows down your bike, and the superfast Neutrinos, who are out of this world. They are a dashing group, full of pizzazz, and they're all in here waiting for you. . . .

E(instein) = mc^2

"Everything should be made as simple as possible, but not simpler."—Albert Einstein (1879–1955)

The original absent-minded professor with his crazy hair and even crazier ideas, Albert Einstein was a superstar scientist who took the world by storm. His revolutionary ideas turned physics—and all of science—upside down.

Physics (and this book) is all about matter and energy. Matter is the stuff that we can see and feel, and energy is the stuff that makes matter do things. Einstein had the genius to see that they are two sides of the same coin, and with some simple math, he brought together the two halves of physics. His famous equation, $E = mc^2$, says that energy (E) is equal to mass (m) multiplied by the speed of light (c) squared, and it shows how a bit of mass can release a tidal wave of energy. As if this wasn't enough, Albert Einstein also had some nifty ideas about how space and time are related. Pretty good for someone who never liked going to school—there's hope for all of us yet!

$E(\text{instein}) = mc^2$

CHAPTER 1
Old School

This robust and gung ho bunch tells us how things in the everyday world interact with one another. They are big, lumbering lumps who love to hang around together. The Old School concerns matter—the stuff that other stuff is made of—and what happens when forces are put into the mix. Without this group, there's no way we could even hope to understand our universe. Even though they are "old school," this gang is showing no signs of slowing down. You could say that these forceful fellows are the ones that really matter!

Mass

Weight

Density

Speed

Acceleration

Force

Inertia

Friction

Gravity

Mass

■ Old School

- A measure of the amount of matter in an object
- Property: even if gravity changes, mass stays the same
- Intimately connected to inertia, but measured in kilograms

As someone who gives things their bulk, I'm a solid and dependable type of guy—a real man of substance. I am the amount of "stuff" that an object is made from. Anything, from the tiniest atom to the most enormous star, has some of me. The only things in the universe without me are pure energy and the waves that carry it.

Want to know how much matter an object has? Check me out! I don't depend on gravity, so I won't go changing (not like weight). For scientists, *massive* doesn't mean huge—dense things cram a lot of mass inside a small space—but usually, the more of me anything has, the bigger it is. Things with a lot of me are very attractive. No, really! The universe's most massive objects have their own alluring force of gravity.

Date of discovery: 1666

- Discoverer: Isaac Newton
- Mass of Earth: 5.976×10^{24}kg
- Mass of Earth's oceans: 1.4×10^{21}kg

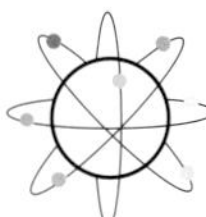

Mass

Weight

■ Old School

- ✷ A downward force that depends on gravity
- ✷ Measured in newtons, not kilograms
- ✷ Don't get him confused with mass or he'll call in the heavies!

I am the man of the moment! From size-zero models to overweight kids, it's all about "weight." But actually, it's not me that people are obsessed with—it's mass. Mass tells you how much matter is in an object, whereas I tell you only what force it exerts (what "push" it has).

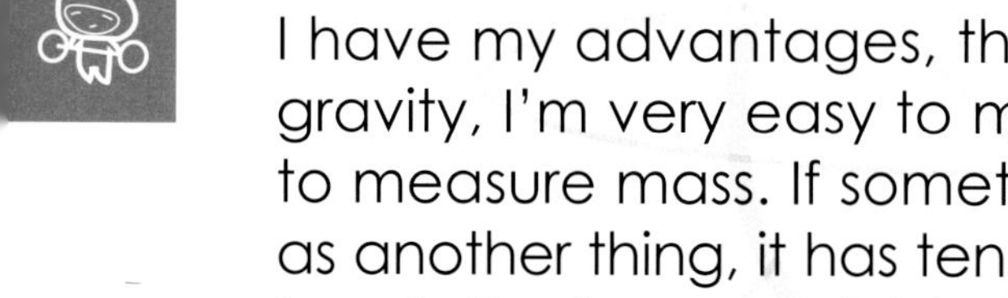

I have my advantages, though—because I depend on gravity, I'm very easy to measure. You can even use me to measure mass. If something weighs ten times as much as another thing, it has ten times as much mass. Easy! But here's the heavyweight part: things can weigh different amounts on different planets. On the Moon, a dumbbell would weigh a mere one sixth of what it does on Earth because of the lower gravity there. In space—away from all gravity—things are weightless.

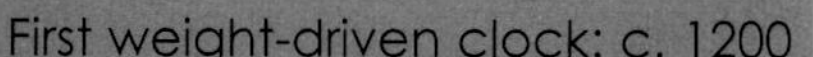
First weight-driven clock: c. 1200

- Weight on Moon: 17% of Earth weight
- Weight on Mars: 38% of Earth weight
- Weight on Jupiter: 213% of Earth weight

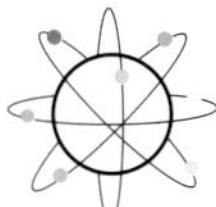

Weight

Density

Old School

- A way of describing how tightly packed a substance is
- The more tightly packed, the denser the substance
- Measured in kilograms per cubic meter

Don't be fooled by my name—I'm not dense. I may be thick, but I'm no dummy. A best buddy of Mass, I'm the measure of how compact materials are. The more mass in anything, the denser it is. I'm just the type of fellow to get you into a tight squeeze, not out of one! Sink or swim, it's all down to me. Less dense things will always rise above more dense things. This is why oil floats on top of water and balloons filled with lighter-than-air helium sail skyward.

Dense things cram a lot of mass into a small space, which makes them feel heavy in your hands. Metals are some of the most tightly packed solids—the elements osmium and iridium are the densest on Earth. Black holes are so dense that their gravity even eats up light.

First density thermometer: 1593

- Density of osmium: 22,610kg/m^3
- Density of iridium: 22,650kg/m^3
- Density of a black hole: 1.8×10^{19}kg/m^3

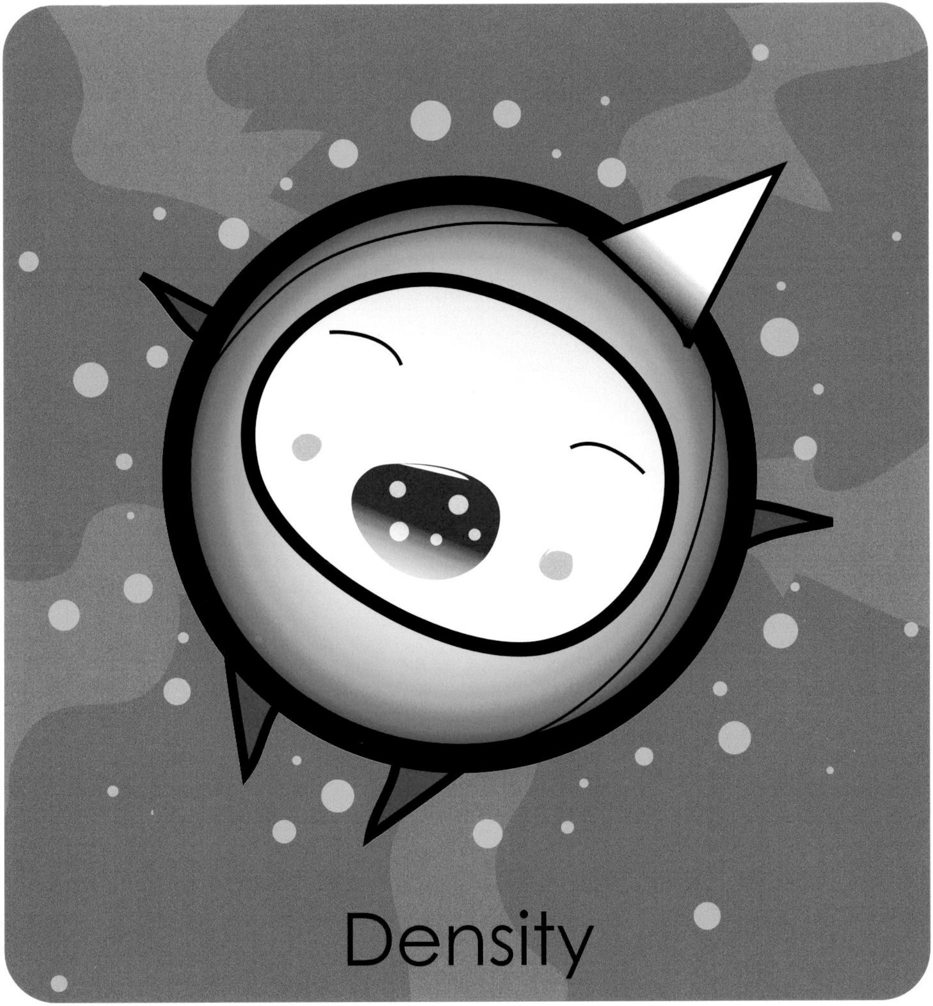

Density

Speed

■ Old School

- Coasts along, covering distance divided by time
- Friction = the only thing that makes Speed lose his cool
- Usually measured in meters per second

Everybody's in a hurry these days, and that makes me a really hot commodity! Internet connection speed, tight deadlines, and speed dating—I'm where it's at. But what's the rush? Chill.

Although I tell you how quickly you can get from point A to point B, I'm a balanced guy and I like things to be paced evenly. If an object has no force pushing it, it stays still or coasts along at the same unchanging speed. Unlike Acceleration, I'm laid-back—you'll get there in the end. No forces, no sweat!

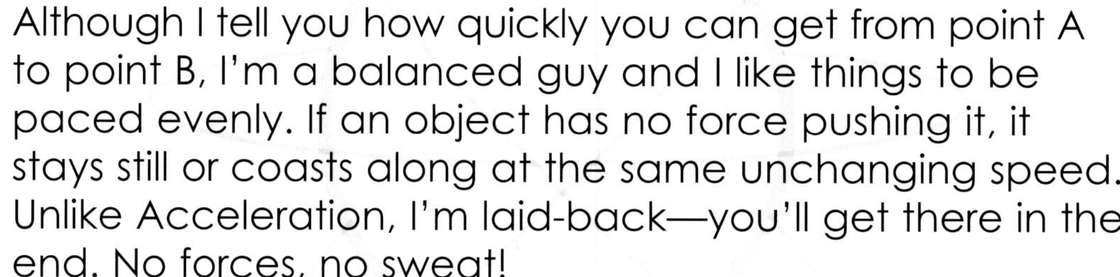

There are lots of ways to measure me. Pilots use "Mach," which compares a jet's speed to the speed of sound. Sailors use "knots," a ropy old-school method.

First land-speed attempt: 1898

- Speed of light: 299,792,458m/s
- Land-speed record: 1,223.65km/h (760.34 mph)
- Free-fall-speed record: 502.1km/h (312 mph)

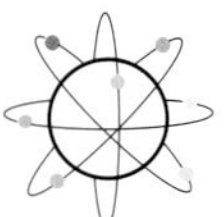

Speed

Acceleration

Old School

- A measure of how quickly things pick up speed
- Not a force, but you feel it as a force
- Measured in meters per second, per second

Forget the need for speed—I've got what it takes to get you going. I'm what makes things pull away from one another, like cars at traffic lights. I'm a total adrenaline junkie who likes to live life in the fast lane.

To fire me up, forces have to be unbalanced, and I always zip off in the direction of the bigger force. You can tell when I'm around, because as I overcome inertia, you feel me pushing you back in your seat. Astronauts feel this as "g forces" ("g" for gravity) as they accelerate against the force of gravity.

The quickest off the mark in the animal kingdom is the cheetah. For speed freaks, drag racers and rockets are the fastest-accelerating human-made machines.

Date of discovery: 1553

- Discoverer: Giambattista Benedetti
- Acceleration of a cheetah: $144m/s^2$
- Acceleration of a drag racer: $2,400m/s^2$

Acceleration

Force

■ Old School

- An overpowering bully measured in newtons
- Gangs up with Mass and Acceleration to push things around
- All of this fellow's actions due to four fundamental forces

I invite you to feel the force! You can't see me. You can't hold me. But you can *feel* me. You can feel me in the grip of your tires on the road, when you kick a ball hard and send it flying, if you've ever struggled to open a can of baked beans, or when reeling around in a square dance. I overcome inertia to push, pull, and twist things around, but I have a tendency to get out of control. When moving things crash, I go haywire and create a mangled wreck.

My golden rule is that for every piece of me produced, there is another equal piece of me produced in the opposite direction. This simple policy stops your feet from sinking into the ground when you walk. It is also how space rockets travel and why running into a wall is a bad idea!

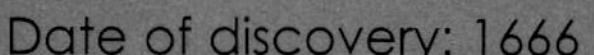

Date of discovery: 1666

- Discoverer: Isaac Newton
- Fundamental forces: gravity, weak force, strong force, electromagnetism

Force

Inertia

Old School

- A two-faced grump measured in newton meters
- Makes objects refuse to be moved at first . . .
- . . . then makes them difficult to stop!

I know I can be difficult, stubborn, and sluggish, but it's my nature. I am an object's resistance to motion. In order to get anything to move, you must first overcome me—and the bigger an object, the less inclined I am to budge. People have inertia, too. It's tricky to get them to do anything when they don't want to—and you know how hard it is to get out of bed in the morning!

But there are two ways for this cookie to crumble, and I have a dangerous flip side. When I get going, I'm like a runaway train—it's hard for me to stop. In this disguise, I go by the name of momentum. Whereas inertia has to do with an object's mass, momentum is what happens when Mass teams up with Speed. Objects happily pass their momentum to another object when they collide.

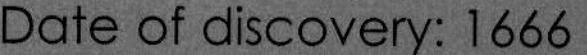

Date of discovery: 1666

- Discoverer: Isaac Newton
- Idea first used: Aristotle, 330 B.C.
- Used to measure mass in zero gravity

Inertia

Friction

■ Old School

- A stick-in-the-mud force who hates all types of movement
- Caused when two surfaces slide past each other
- Takes orders from Entropy and is measured in newtons

I'm a fly in the ointment, a master of mayhem, and a frequent cause of aggravation. My disruptive force makes energy lose its usefulness, wears out mechanical parts, and generates heat in moving things and electrical components. Don't talk to me about that smoothie Speed—I'm determined to slow him down! I'm also a secret agent for Entropy, a member of the Hot Stuff crew and the universe's king of chaos. By generating excess heat, I take useful energy—like kinetic energy—out of a system and spread it around.

Things may be a bit of a drag when I'm around, but don't think I'm good for nothing. Without me, the world would be a very slippery place—your shoes wouldn't grip the ground and the brakes on cars and bikes would be useless. You need me more than you know it!

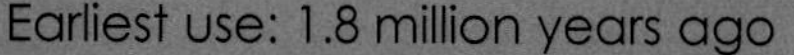

Earliest use: 1.8 million years ago

- Slipperiest stuff: near-frictionless carbon
- Stickiest stuff: a glue made by mollusks
- Drag on a car at 100km/h (60 mph): around 280 N

Friction

Gravity

Old School

- The force of attraction between two objects
- A fundamental force that never quite disappears
- The gravity of huge galaxies can actually bend light!

I am a mystical mover and shaker, and my field of operations is the vastness of space. A universal fixer, I hold Earth together, keep the planets in their orbits, and make stars form, as well as do more mundane tasks such as keeping your feet on the ground. I do my work over very long distances, with no strings attached.

I was the first of the four fundamental forces to be found. (We are the forces that do the universe's work and keep things ticking.) I combine with mass to keep you pinned down and stop you from jumping too high. I am the weakest of the four, but you still keep falling for me! Space rockets must use acceleration in order to escape me. I power water wheels, roller coasters, and grandfather clocks—and I'm pretty essential for skydivers, too!

Date of discovery: 1666

- Discoverer: Isaac Newton
- Range: infinite
- Carrier: graviton (unobserved)

Gravity

CHAPTER 2

Hot Stuff

If you're in need of a little oomph, look no further! This high-octane group is literally bursting with pep and a lust for life. These guys get things done for you and provide the necessary drive to start things moving and growing on Earth. Scientists know an awful lot about how this team interacts with one another, but truth be told, energy is still mysterious stuff. This group is from the other side of the tracks compared to the matter meatheads of the Old School gang, and their high spirits and verve make them an entirely different prospect. . . .

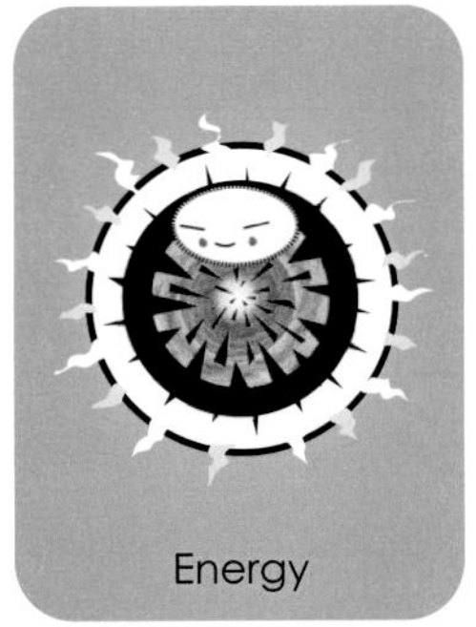
Energy

Potential Energy

Kinetic Energy

Entropy

Vacuum

Blackbody Radiation

Energy

Hot Stuff

- Hot stuff that has a burning desire to get things done
- The amount of energy and mass in the universe = constant
- Measured in joules or calories in food

Mighty and morphing, I exist in many guises and make the universe tick. My incredible ability to slide effortlessly among my different forms drives nature and machines alike. I give you your get-up-and-go and enable plants to grow and your brain to think; engines turn potential energy (fuel) and kinetic energy (motion) into power. Humans worship me and start wars over the means to my production but still waste vast amounts of me every day.

Most of the energy on Earth comes from the Sun, which gives off more energy in one second than all of the world's most powerful nuclear reactors release in one year! I am everything there is. Einstein said that even matter—the stuff that you, me, and everything else is made of—is just a supercondensed form of me. Neat, huh?

Date of discovery: 1823

- Discoverer: Sadi Carnot
- Energy used in U.S. per year: 9×10^{19} J
- Power output of the Sun: 4×10^{26} J/s

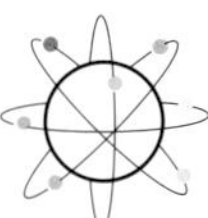

Energy

Potential Energy

Hot Stuff

- Stored energy, or "energy on tap"
- Can be turned into kinetic energy
- High-strung, ready to go off, and measured in joules

Like a tiger ready to pounce, I'm poised, ready for action, and raring to go. I am the energy in a stretched catapult, a coiled spring, a roller coaster at the top of a drop, a candy bar, and a fully charged battery.

I literally have lots of potential. I am stored energy that can be converted into other forms. Like money, I'm described by where I am stored. But instead of cash, checks, gold, and jewelry, I come as elastic, gravitational, electrical, and chemical potential energy. Springs use stored elastic energy to drive mechanisms such as wind-up watches. Many things are powered by objects falling under gravity. Batteries power electrical devices, and the chemical energy stored in the sugar of a soft drink will have you bouncing off the ceiling!

Date of discovery: 1850s

- Discoverer: William Rankine
- Highest roller-coaster drop: 139m (456 ft.)
- Energy in 100g (3.5 oz.) of chocolate: 2000 kJ

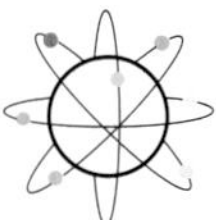

Potential Energy

Kinetic Energy

Hot Stuff

- A dynamic character who gives pizzazz to things on the move
- Heat = the kinetic energy of a substance's molecules
- Depends on mass and speed and is measured in joules

I am the buzz that speed freaks chase. I'm what happens when mass gets into motion. I adore acceleration—as a thing picks up speed, it gains kinetic energy. Skydivers falling in the sky can almost feel their potential energy changing into me by the second as the ground rushes toward them.

I'm used to make electricity, and I power all types of machines. All of this gusto can come at a cost, though. I'm the thing that kills people in car accidents because I depend on speed squared—travel twice as fast, and you have four times as much of me. I am genuinely hot stuff. The hotter an object gets, the more internal energy its molecules gain and the more they jostle around. This is one of the ways that entropy decreases my usefulness.

Date of discovery: 1829

- Discoverer: Gaspard-Gustave de Coriolis
- Energy of a nuclear bomb: 4×10^{15} J
- Power of a hurricane: 1.3×10^{17} J/day

Kinetic Energy

Entropy

Hot Stuff

- The measure of disorder in the universe
- A master of disaster and the enemy of all machines
- The perfect excuse for never cleaning your bedroom!

I am the king of chaos—a mixed-up prankster who makes sure that energy always changes from useful forms to messed-up, spread-out forms. A renowned troublemaker, I'm the reason why things break and burn out, and I'll get you, too, in the end. Ultimately, I'll cause your body's cells to degrade and stop working properly and you'll die.

I always increase, and I work in one direction only—things NEVER get neater unless you put some effort in. Gasoline has lots of potential energy tied up in its arrangement of atoms, but when it explodes, this stored energy is spread out irreversibly. The chaos has increased, so there's more of me. Hurrah! In short, I create havoc. This is why it's pointless cleaning your room—because the universe is working against you. Next time, try that as an excuse!

Date of discovery: 1865

- Discoverer: Rudolf Clausius
- Heat that fire walkers withstand: 650°C (1,200°F)
- Lowest boiling point: –269°C/–452°F (helium)

Entropy

Vacuum

Hot Stuff

- An empty void where there is no stuff hanging around
- With no matter around, no friction to slow things down
- A complete sucker used in high-tech physics experiments

I'm a riddle. I am what I'm not. A blank space without a crumb of matter. Diddly-squat. Ancient scientists thought that I was impossible—how could nothing be something? But it's only away from the influence of mass and matter that the universe approaches perfection. I cancel out friction so that light can travel at its theoretical fastest.

I clean your home, freeze-dry and vacuum-pack food for freshness, and keep your drinks hot or cold inside thermoses. But step outside a spacecraft in outer space and I'll suck the life out of you in a few minutes. My lack of pressure will also boil your bodily fluids. Astronauts wear pressurized suits to stop this from happening. But even in the cold emptiness of space, there's a tiny flicker of restless energy. You might get something from nothing after all!

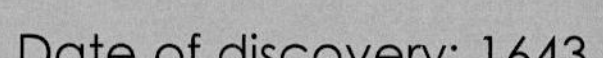

Date of discovery: 1643

- Discoverer: Evangelista Torricelli
- Pressure in outer space: 10^{-16} torr
- Emptiest artificial vacuum: 10^{-13} torr

Vacuum

Blackbody Radiation

Hot Stuff

- A ninjalike shadow who swallows and slays the Light Crew
- Dark and mysterious, a heat monitor for the universe
- Produces radiation that depends only on his heat

I am a master of the dark arts. When an object is pure black like me, it absorbs all of the light that hits it and radiates it back as heat. My special heat "signature" makes me easy to spot and has helped scientists learn about energy's strange ways. I am the reason why black things heat up and shiny white objects stay cool.

In hot countries, it's a good idea to wear light colors—black clothes may look hip, but they certainly won't keep you cool! I'm not just about gobbling up energy, though—blackbodies also give off heat much more easily than nonabsorbing white or silvery bodies. This is why hot things, such as car radiators, get painted black.

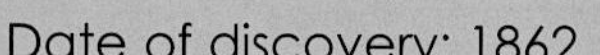

Date of discovery: 1862

- Discoverer: Gustav Kirchhoff
- Most unusual blackbodies (BB): hot stars
- "Best" BB: carbon (absorbs 97% of light)

Blackbody Radiation

CHAPTER 3

Wave Gang

This small group of movers and shakers creates a big splash wherever it goes. A harmonious bunch, they fill the universe with light and sound as they transport energy from place to place. The Wave Gang warps space to make this happen, but they themselves don't travel—they just send the Hot Stuff crew along on the wing. Sometimes you can actually see the waves transporting energy—think of water waves or earthquakes—but other times you only feel the effect of the energy, such as when a blast of sound hits you.

Water Wave

Sound

Earthquake

Frequency

Amplitude

Laser

Analogue

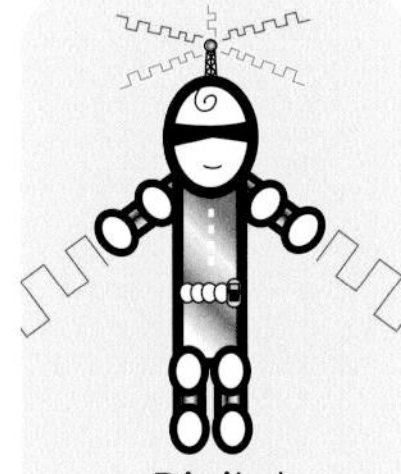

Digital

Water Wave

Wave Gang

- A totally rad method for energy to travel from point A to point B
- Uses up-and-down movements
- A choppy fellow, closely related to Frequency and Amplitude

Aloha! I've never had any qualms about rocking the boat—it's my purpose in life, man. I'm a thrill-seeking surfer dude who's out to make a few waves! One thing you gotta understand about me is that I ain't going nowhere. I'm just a way for energy to get around. I move only up and down, like a person at a football game doing the wave. No one in the crowd actually changes seats, but the wave (like energy) travels around the stadium. The more energy I carry, the higher my peaks.

Surface waves are made by the wind whipping up the water. Deeper water waves are caused by the Moon's gravity pulling on ocean water. This energy can be used to generate electric currents. Dropping in on a big swell is bodacious, but my talent for seasickness is bogus!

Earliest use of wave power: 1799

- Asian tsunami death toll (2004): 300,000 people
- Largest earthquake: N. Sumatra, Indonesia (8.9 on the Richter scale)
- Height of killer waves: 15m (49 ft.)

Water Wave

Sound

Wave Gang

- Energy waves that are detected by your eardrums
- Travels by vibrations in matter—via longitudinal waves
- Can't travel in a vacuum—no one can hear you scream in space!

I surround you—no matter where you go, I'm there, vibrating in your ears. Even the quietest sound moves your eardrums. This is a good thing because it lets you talk to other people and listen to the world's beautiful noises. Kids really love me, but older folks tend to like me less and complain about me more.

I get from place to place by causing small disturbances that are passed along in the same way that pushes and shoves move you through a crowd of people. Watch a loudspeaker at work and you'll see how the speaker cone pushes and pulls the air around it. I travel pretty fast, but supersonic jets can "break the sound barrier," releasing huge amounts of energy in a sonic boom. Thunder is a natural sonic boom.

Sound barrier broken: 1947

- Speed of sound: 330m/s
- Range of human hearing: 20–20,000 Hz
- Loudest sound recorded: Volcano eruption in Krakatau, Indonesia (1883)

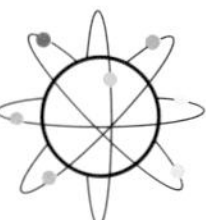

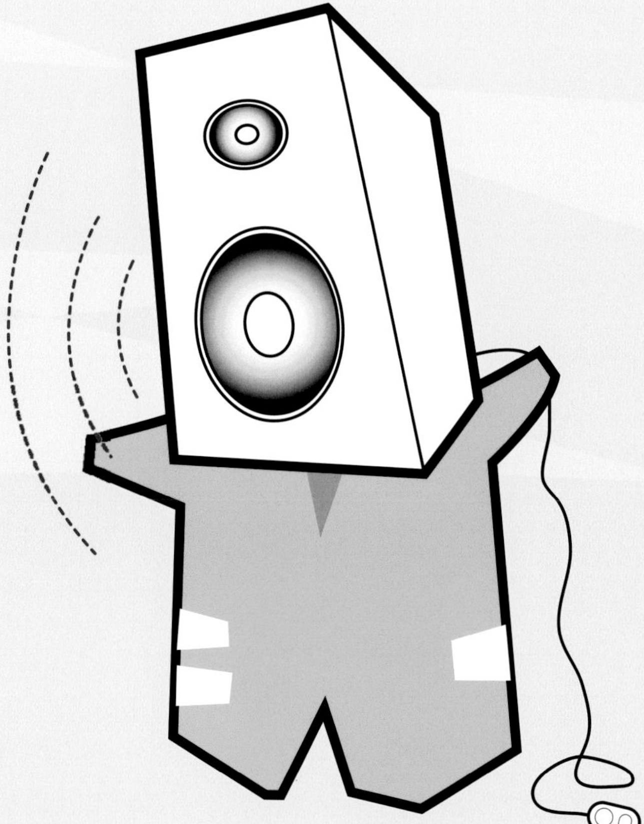

Sound

Earthquake

Wave Gang

- A sudden release of stored energy that shakes the ground
- Most of the world's quakes = in the Pacific Ocean's "Ring of Fire"
- Tremors measured on the Richter or Moment scales

Swift and deadly, I strike without warning, spreading chaos and disaster. I break Earth like a cookie, causing landslides, avalanches, fires, mudflows, and tsunamis. Minor quakes often pass harmlessly, but when I come to town in a major way, I really cause a stir. My seismic waves tear up roads like ribbons and flatten buildings.

I occur when friction builds up between huge masses of Earth's crust, around 10km (6 mi.) below the surface. When this stored energy is released, the crust leaps and buckles. Most of the energy that I generate goes into overcoming friction. But the rest throws up the ground in a series of waves. P waves (primary, such as sound waves) are compression waves and travel the fastest. S waves (secondary, such as water waves) are tremors and arrive later.

First earthquake detector: A.D. 132

- Major quakes per year: 1,500
- Biggest quake: Niebla, Chile (1960)
- Deadliest quake: Shaanxi, China (1556)

Earthquake

Frequency

Wave Gang

- The amount of repeating wave patterns per unit of time
- Related to the pitch of sound and the energy of the Light Crew
- Measured in hertz

I'm the most important measure of any wave. I am the one that counts because I tell you how many cycles—or identical patterns of waves—pass a point in a given time. The higher I am, the more peaks and troughs I get through the gate every second. This is measured in hertz, but—before you ask—no, it doesn't "hertz"!

Generally speaking, the greater the frequency, the more energy the waves carry and the straighter the line they travel in. This is especially true of the Light Crew. High-frequency photons can burn and damage cells inside your body. Infrasound is low-frequency rumbles, such as whale songs, which travel for miles. Ultrasound, above the range of human hearing, can boil an egg but is also used to make pictures of babies in the womb.

Earliest use of hertz: 1930

- Named after Heinrich Hertz
- 1 Hz = 1 cycle per second
- Household electricity: 50 Hz

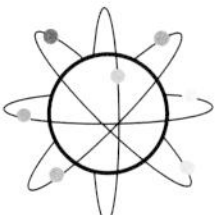

Frequency

Amplitude

Wave Gang

- This rowdy rabble-rouser = a property of all waves
- The height of the maximum disturbance in a wave cycle
- The more amplitude a wave has, the more energy it carries

I love to let my hair down and raise the roof. I'm a party animal, and the powerful effects I have on waves keep the neighborhood awake at night. I'm the measure of a wave's movement—usually taken from its midpoint, where the wave is at rest, to the crest—so I can be used to describe any wave that you can imagine.

I'm all about agitation and upset. With water waves, the higher the wave, the more energy it carries and the bigger the thrill to ride it. With sound, increasing me makes the wave louder. When the electromagnetic waves of the Light Crew get just a smidgen more of me, they get brighter. The old codger Analogue uses me to transmit information in waves. He encodes messages into AM radio waves by altering the height of the signals.

First AM radio transmission: 1906

- AM inventor: Reginald Fessenden
- Long wave: 153–279 kHz
- Medium wave: 520–1,610 kHz

Amplitude

Laser

Wave Gang

- Fully focused energy in a fine-tuned light beam
- LASER = Light Amplification by Stimulated Emission of Radiation
- Einstein's idea in 1917; now plays music and stitches up muscles

Highly honed and toned and at the peak of my game, I make light work of any task! Be it surgery or industrial metalwork, I always cut through to the heart of the matter. Unlike other light sources, I'm completely focused. I use a unique method to whip the waves in my beams into line and keep them tight and under control.

Unlike the rest of the Wave Gang, I've been invented by physicists. I come in all sizes, from tiny components in electronic circuit boards to warehouse-size units for atom smashing. I'm proud to say that I'm spectacularly useful! Not only do I read your CDs and DVDs, but I also check bar codes on products, print your documents, and protect your valuables. I can even undertake tricky eye operations without batting an eyelid!

Earliest known use: 1960

- Inventor: Theodore Maiman
- Max. depth of steel-cutting laser: 6cm (2 in.)
- Temperature of a steel cutter: 5,000°C (9,000°F)

Laser

Analogue

Wave Gang

- A way of using carrier waves to transmit information
- Used for TV and radio broadcasts and old-school sounds
- Despite what the purists say, this old fellow is prone to errors. . . .

I'm a scratchy old fool, but I make no apologies. I have had a long and illustrious career in broadcasting, so it feels a little sad as the modern world chooses the fashionable Digital over me. Nevertheless, I prefer to remain a specialist—and I'm not without my advantages.

I am the original way of sending information from one place to another, using waves. The trick is to encode information onto "carrier waves" such as radio waves or electric currents. This new "modulated" wave has peaks and troughs that mirror the original message. It can be decoded to extract the info, but pieces of the wave often go missing. My first use was in telephones. Later came radio, TV, and vinyl records. Music lovers prefer me to digital because I'm more faithful to the original sound.

First patented telephone: 1876

- First phone call: Antonio Meucci (1854)
- First radio relay: Mahlon Loomis (1872)
- First LP record: RCA Victor (1930)

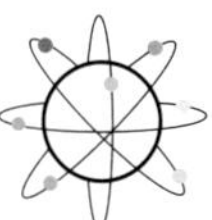

Analogue

Digital

Wave Gang

- An information-encoding method that plays a numbers game
- Despite its critics, digital = noise free, quick, and easy
- Has led to the most incredible explosion of technology

The digital revolution has happened, my friends! No longer will your music be plagued with horrible hisses! No more will mysterious pings and pops ruin your phone calls! I'm not prone to errors because I turn info into numbers. You can count on me—after all, I'm just a stream of zeros and ones.

The key to my mastery is sampling. Instead of grafting all of the information onto a carrier wave like that fuddy-duddy Analogue, I sample the info at different points. Each point gives you a value that can be encoded as a string of "on" (one) or "off" (zero) signals. This makes the decoder's job much easier and means that the info gets through crisply—which is why I'm used for cell phones, TVs, computers, CDs, DVDs, and satellite systems.

Date of discovery: 1701

- First digital computer: Z3 (1941)
- First communications satellite: SCORE (1958)
- First CD: Philips and Sony (1982)

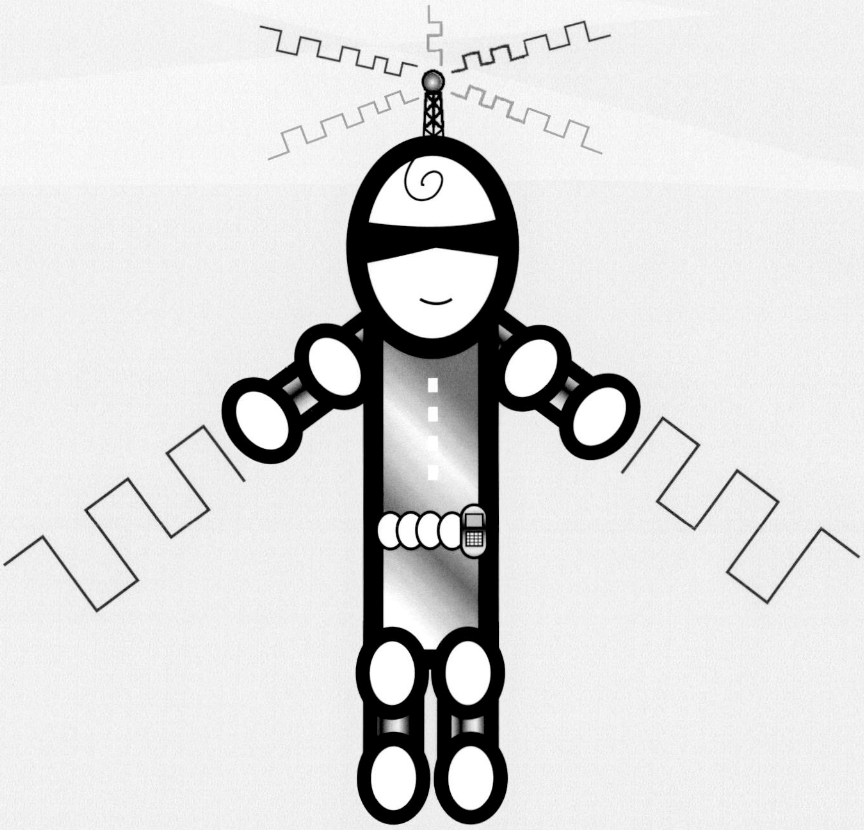

Digital

CHAPTER 4

Light Crew

This bunch of turbocharged twinkle toes are the fastest things in the universe. Completely massless, they weigh nothing and have the uncanny ability to act like both particles and waves. Unlike other waves, however, this bright bunch doesn't need materials to carry it along. These children of the Sun travel express through the vacuum of space at the speed of light. Together, the Light Crew makes up an electromagnetic spectrum, which means that this colorful group is essentially all the same—photons with differing amounts of energy.

Radio Wave

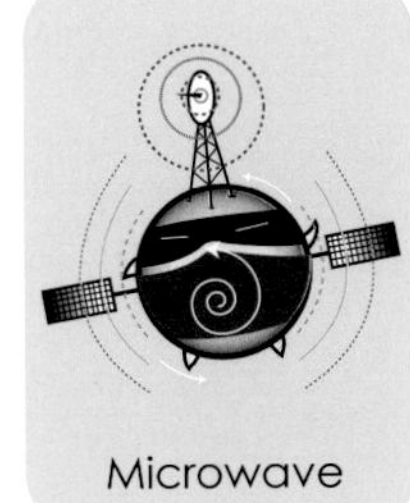
Microwave

Infrared

Light

Ultraviolet

X-ray

Gamma Ray

Radio Wave

Light Crew

- Old-school "wireless" technology, produced in a wide band
- The lowest-frequency member of the Light Crew
- The atmosphere = "invisible" to radio—it sails straight through

I am the workhorse of the airwaves, and I'm so useful that governments strictly regulate my use. Made by whipping electrons up into a frenzy in a thin wire, I am bounced around the world carrying TV and radio transmissions, wireless Internet, and all of your phone calls and text messages. Despite the bad press, I'm completely harmless and won't fry your brain when you press your cell phone against your sweaty ear.

Sparks and electrical noise interfere with transmitting me cleanly—which is why your radio clicks when you turn on a light—but because I can travel out across space, astronomers go gaga for me. Radio telescopes listen in to the pops and crackles of invisible galaxies and search for signs of life in the universe. I'm also used for weather forecasting, spacecraft guidance, and radar.

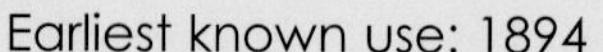

Earliest known use: 1894

- First broadcast: Guglielmo Marconi (1901)
- International distress signal (air): 121.5 MHz
- Frequency band: 30 KHz–300 GHz

Radio Wave

Microwave

Light Crew

- High-frequency radio wave that has a deep love of water
- Produced in devices called klystrons
- Gets all sorts of molecules hot under the collar

I'm no ordinary radio wave. In fact, I am the top rank of the radio-frequency band. With my ability to excite water, fats, and sugar molecules, I have single-handedly invented a whole new food industry: the microwave meal! I put molecules in a whirl—when they feel me, they cannot help rotating. As they jostle around, they transfer their motion to one another, increasing the food's internal kinetic energy and heating it up.

Microwave ovens are shielded by metal so that I don't cook everything in the kitchen. I'm not that dangerous—just don't try to dry your pets with me! I'm sneaky, too—I'm used by spy satellites and to trap speeding drivers. But stealth bombers are invisible to me, so they fly right under my prying eyes.

Date of discovery: 1888

- Discoverer: Heinrich Hertz
- Microwave-oven frequency: 2,450 MHz
- Frequency band: 300 MHz–300 GHz

Microwave

Infrared

Light Crew

- Hot things give off infrared, but infrared not the same as heat
- Most infrared from the Sun blocked by Earth's atmosphere
- Used by remote controls to zap your wishes invisibly

You can run, but you can't hide. I'm the original heat seeker, and I'm out to give you a good grilling! Invisible to human eyes, I'm given off by hot things. This makes me an excellent ally if you're into the game of seek and destroy. Even in the dark of the night, my telltale signature shines through.

On the battlefield, where targets are often far away, moving fast, or hidden, the military locks its missiles onto my signal. Night Vision goggles enhance poor light by using infrared, making it easy to spot escaping people. Even some deadly snakes hunt at night using infrared vision. But I can also be used to save people. Thermal-imaging cameras are used by rescue services to search for bodies in rubble and by firefighters to locate the heart of a blaze.

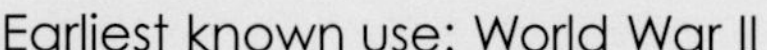
Earliest known use: World War II

- Average human body temperature: 37°C (98.6°F)
- Number of infrared "pit" organs on a snake: 20
- Frequency band: 3×10^5–4×10^8 GHz

Infrared

Light

Light Crew

- Electromagnetic energy detected by your eyes
- White light = made up of the rainbow spectrum of colors
- Human behavior patterns changed forever by the light bulb

Let there be *me*! And the world became a reality. . . . I control what the world looks like because I am what you see when you look at it. You and I have had a long relationship—because most of the energy coming from the Sun is in my frequency band, it is no coincidence that your eyes have evolved to be sensitive to me.

Plants use my energy to help them grow, but people love me so much that they have canceled the night. They can no longer see the stars in their cities, but the cities' bright lights can be seen from outer space. Optical fibers now carry your phone calls, coding your conversations into pulses of light. Superspeedy optical computers might soon put semiconductors out of work, getting the job done in the blink of an eye. The future's bright—it's blindingly obvious!

Date of discovery: 1670s

- Discoverer: Isaac Newton
- Time to get "night vision": 5–10 minutes
- Frequency band: 3.8–7.5 x 10^8 GHz

Light

Ultraviolet

Light Crew

- Sunburn kings from space, divided into UVA, UVB, and UVC
- The most energetic ultraviolet rays able to blind you
- Most of these nasty horrors stopped by Earth's ozone layer

I am radiation for Sun worshipers. Eagerly racing from the Sun, I love nothing better than fresh bodies laid out on a beach, slathered in coconut oil.

A little of me is a good thing—I lift the clouds and cheer you up if you're feeling down—but a little too much and I start to tinker with the DNA in your cells. I break chemical bonds, unleashing reactive molecules that can cause skin cancer. A pigment in skin called melanin darkens to give more protection against me, but if it wasn't for the ozone layer, I would toast you and turn Earth into a barren desert. I am used in insect zappers and also to sterilize drinking water. Blacklights are UV lights that can spot forged money, make your teeth shine like a crazy fool . . . and show off your dandruff!

Date of discovery: 1801

- Discoverer: Johann Wilhelm Ritter
- Scorpions glow deadly yellow in UV
- Frequency band: 7.5×10^{8}–3×10^{10} GHz

Ultraviolet

X-ray

Light Crew

- High-energy radiation that can cause—and cure—cancer
- Lead-lined aprons worn by radiologists to protect them
- Exotic and extreme, the "x" actually stands for "unknown"!

I am an electromagnetic peeping Tom who finds it irresistible to peek inside things. I'm so keyed up and exuberant that I can't help slipping inside materials to take a look. Although I'm dangerous company, my talent for spying makes me useful in medicine and industry—I'm a star with that all-important "x" factor!

I'm made when streams of high-energy electrons slam into a metal target. My most famous use is in hospitals, where I look for broken bones. I zap straight through soft tissue, so bones show up as ghostly skeletons on photographic paper. In 1999, the Chandra X-ray Observatory in Massachusetts tuned in to x-rays from outer space to reveal a scary, unseen universe where black holes tear stars apart and neutron stars blow themselves to pieces.

Date of discovery: 1895

- Discoverer: Wilhelm Röntgen
- Most powerful x-ray source: quasars
- Frequency band: 3×10^{10}–10^{13} GHz

X-ray

Gamma Ray

Light Crew

- A lethal form of nuclear radiation, stopped only by thick lead
- The shortest wavelength and highest-energy photon
- The main cause of radiation sickness

Fresh from the fire of nuclear reactions, I'll fry you to a crisp. I'm mean, lean, and full of beans—I travel at the speed of light and cut right through any material as if it wasn't there. It takes a great thickness of lead to stop me. Because of this, I'm extremely dangerous and can cause serious damage to humans. Most of the casualties in a nuclear bomb blast are my fault.

Gamma-ray detectors were put into space in the 1960s to spy on illegal nuclear tests. What they discovered instead were the universe's most violent explosions—gamma-ray bursts. These come from outside our galaxy around once each day, but scientists can't agree on what they are. It's not all about destruction, though—I sterilize food and kill off cancer cells. . . . Oh, maybe it is after all!

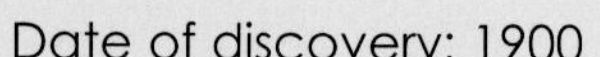

Date of discovery: 1900

- Discoverer: Paul Villard
- First gamma-ray telescope: 1961
- Frequency band: greater than 10^{14} GHz

Gamma Ray

CHAPTER 5

Atom Family

The Atom Family is a thoroughly modern bunch with many talents. Fun loving and bouncy, at last count there were more than 150 of them. What has particle physicists scratching their heads is how they are all related, as some family members can change into other ones. Some are "fundamental particles," which means that they cannot be broken down into smaller particles. But all of the members of the Atom Family are very small. Ruled over by strong and weak forces, surprising things happen to them that are completely out of the ordinary.

Atom

Electron

Proton

Neutron

Quark

Neutrino

Higgs Boson

Strong Force

Antimatter

Atom

Atom Family

- All matter in the universe made up of this intriguing fellow
- 117 different types of atoms known to science
- A stable character with a very long history

I am all around you—every object that you pick up or sit on is made of me, and even the air that you breathe is full of me. But I'm so small that you could hide 500,000 of me behind a single human hair with room to spare. No wonder it took scientists 100 years to track me down!

I am the "Big Daddy" of the Atom Family. I fit a lot inside me, but mostly I'm empty space. Protons and neutrons squeeze inside my tiny central nucleus, and electrons orbit around it. I'm very happy to lose or share electrons in chemical reactions with other atoms. To break me open is easy—you do it every time you turn on the TV—but splitting my nucleus is ridiculously hard and requires lots of energy. This is why atoms made at the start of time are still around today. I'm gonna live forever!

Date of discovery: 1803

- Discoverers: John Dalton; Niels Bohr (1913)
- Average size: 1.06×10^{-10}m
- Atomic number = number of protons in nucleus

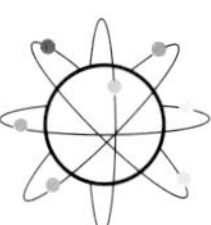

Atom

Electron

Atom Family

- Fundamental particle found orbiting an atom's nucleus
- Always as many electrons as protons in an atom
- A feather-light tyke that packs a tremendous punch

I'm a negative particle. Nothing wrong with that. A bit of negativity is healthy. I normally zip around the outer regions of an atom. I always return and I can't help it—with a negative charge equal to a proton's positive charge, I am constantly drawn toward the nucleus. However, you'll never pin me down—I'm so fast that I exist in a blur.

I give an atom its personality, but I'm only loosely attached, and I love to buzz off and do my own thing, which often gets me involved in chemical reactions. Life must have been pretty dull before humans learned to use me. In a mere 100 years, I've supercharged the modern world. I make all of your electrical gadgets work, from TVs to MP3 players. I'm also used in electron microscopes. These high-tech snoops can see inside the tiny world of the atom.

Date of discovery: 1897

- Discoverer: J. J. Thomson
- Group: lepton
- Mass: 9.109×10^{-31}kg

Electron

Proton

Atom Family

- Subatomic particle found in the nucleus of an atom
- Loves to be at the center of things
- Not a fundamental particle—made up of quarks

A big, chunky hunk of positivity, I hang out in the middle of an atom—the nucleus. The nucleus is one of the smallest places imaginable. It's not so great for someone who's as antisocial as me—I can't bear to be around other protons. However, in spite of the repulsion among us, there I am, squished up tightly and rammed together by Strong Force and his neutron police.

I'm a big fellow, around 2,000 times bigger than an electron and just as many times less crazy, so you won't see me shooting all over the place making and breaking alliances. I am much more responsible—I'm what gives an atom its identity. There are 117 different types of atoms, called elements, and they are all unique, thanks to me. Hydrogen is the smallest, with only one proton.

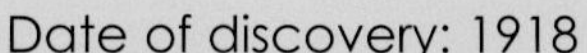

Date of discovery: 1918

- Discoverer: Ernest Rutherford
- Mass: 1.673×10^{-27}kg
- Made of two "U" quarks and one "D" quark

Proton

Neutron

Atom Family

- This fat fellow = the last piece of the atomic jigsaw puzzle
- Only affected by the strong force and gravity
- Made up of quarks and is the key to nuclear chain reactions

No jokes about my size, please. Yes, I am heavy and somewhat dull, but I am the glue that holds an atom's nucleus together. It is cramped up tightly with protons, and I am a calming influence—without me, the unruly protons would repel one another and fly off to infinity. Along with the protons, I beef up atoms and give them mass. There are often more neutrons than protons in a nucleus, but sometimes even a few more of us squeeze in, making heavier (and often radioactive) isotopes.

My name gives away the game. I am entirely neutral and unaffected by electromagnetism. Extract me from the nucleus and fire me at the heart of an atom, and it splits apart. This causes the violent chain reactions that are used in nuclear reactors and atom bombs.

Date of discovery: 1932

- Discoverer: James Chadwick
- Rest mass: 1.674×10^{-27}kg
- Made of one "U" quark and two "D" quarks

Neutron

Quark

Atom Family

- A flavorful bunch of fundamental particles
- Forms larger subatomic particles such as neutrons and protons
- "Quark" not a seagull noise—it rhymes with "pork"

Tiny and gentle, we are a gang of six fun-loving fundamental particles. Along with electrons and neutrinos, we are the basic building blocks of matter, but we exist at an even deeper level, invisible to light and almost always hidden from detection. We hide in the shadows in the tightest spaces in the universe—inside protons and neutrons in the nuclei of atoms.

We come in six different "flavors" called Up, Down, Top, Bottom, Strange, and Charm. That may sound to you as if we're just missing Dopey to complete the seven dwarfs, but we don't want to hear your wisecracks! We hang out in groups of two or three, and we can swap flavors among us—with the help of the weak force. That makes it tough to find out anything solid about us.

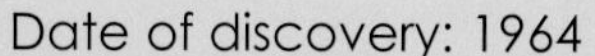

Date of discovery: 1964

- Discoverer: Murray Gell-Mann
- Size: 1×10^{-18}m (the largest)
- 2 quarks = 1 meson; 3 quarks = 1 baryon

Quark

Neutrino

Atom Family

- Ludicrously slippery fundamental particles in the lepton group
- These energetic particles produced in nuclear reactions
- Are almost impossible to spot and travel close to the speed of light

Up, up, and away! We are the mavericks of the Atom Family. Trillions upon trillions of us stream off the Sun every second, produced by the nuclear reactions inside its core. We move like greased lightning and we're just as slick—almost every single one of us sails clean through Earth without hitting anything. More than 50 trillion neutrinos whiz through your body each second, but you don't feel a thing—with almost no mass and no electrical charge, we're virtually undetectable.

Scientists studying reactions in the Sun use vast vats of dry-cleaning fluid buried inside deep mine shafts to watch for us. Tiny puffs of energy in the liquid signal our passing. It took 26 years to find us; in theory, we come in three "flavors," but so far, only one has been spotted.

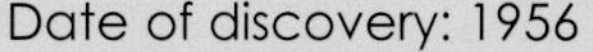

Date of discovery: 1956

- Discoverers: Wolfgang Pauli; Reines & Cowan
- Named by Enrico Fermi
- Mass: currently too small to measure

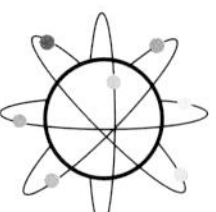

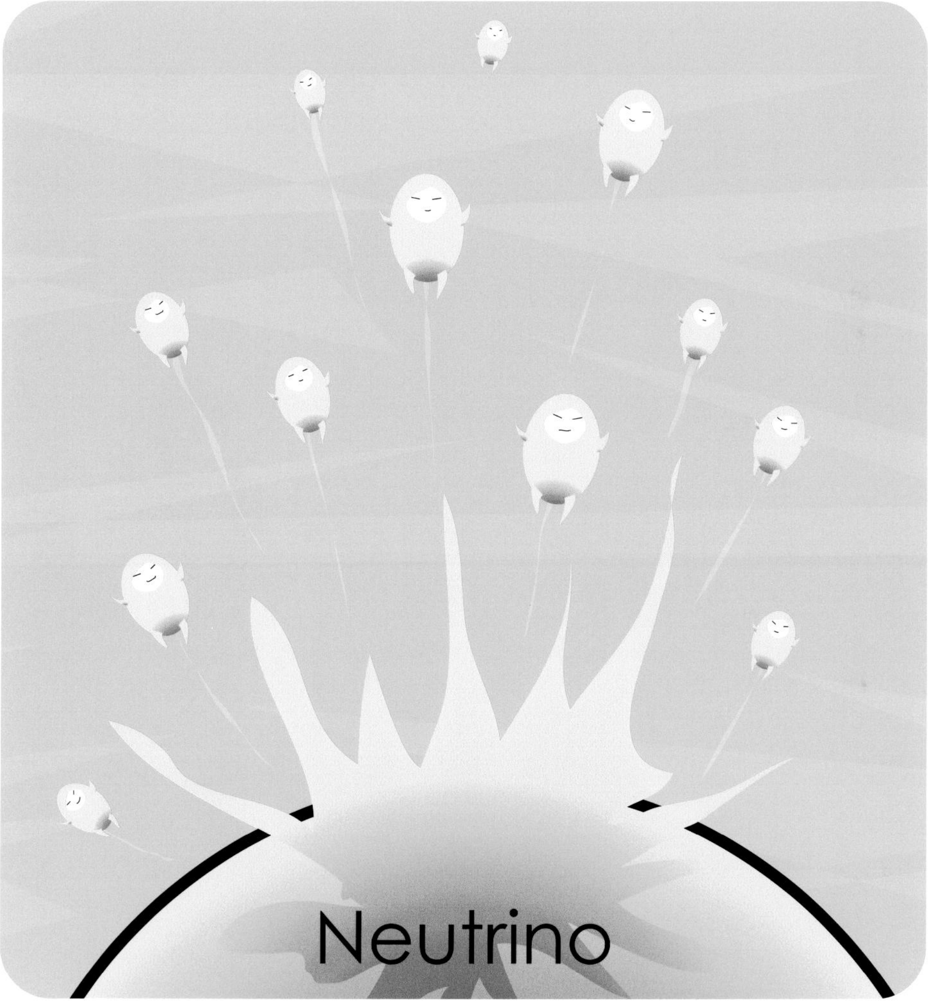

Neutrino

Higgs Boson

Atom Family

- Thought to be the particle that gives mass to matter
- The subject of physics's greatest manhunt
- No one certain that this little fellow exists at all

Extremely shy and retiring, I've played hide-and-seek with the greatest minds in physics for more than 40 years. I'm the one that got away! Theoretical scientists are desperate to find me because I am the missing link in all of their theories about matter.

They think that I cluster around particles of matter, giving them mass. It's funny how something as unobtrusive as me could give mass to anything, but this idea explains where mass comes from and why it's always positive. Physicists also think that I might be the reason why there's more matter than antimatter in the universe. They are so eager to find me that they've built a hugely expensive 27-km (17-mi.)-long proton-smashing machine called the large hadron collider (LHC) in Geneva, Switzerland. The hunt is on!

As yet unobserved

- Proposed by Peter Higgs
- AKA the "God particle"
- Energy of LHC beam: 350 MJ

Higgs Boson

Strong Force

Atom Family

- The force of attraction that holds an atom's nucleus together
- The strongest of the four fundamental forces
- Responsible for nasty radioactivity such as alpha particles

I am the universe's strongman. The Magnificent! The Unbeatable! I am more than 100 times stronger than electromagnetism and one million times stronger than the weak force, and without me there'd be no atoms.

Inside an atom's nucleus, a tremendous battle is going on between me and the force of electromagnetism. This force makes positively charged protons repel one another violently, but I slave tirelessly to keep it all together—without me, protons would hurtle off into infinity. My special interaction makes them attractive to one another, but it works only over very small distances. It's really difficult to hold together the nucleus of big atoms, and sometimes it gets too much. When my powers break down, the nucleus splits, releasing radioactive alpha particles.

Date of discovery: 1934

- Discoverer: Hideki Yukawa
- Range: 10^{-15}m
- Carrier: gluon particle

Strong Force

Antimatter

Atom Family

- The opposite of normal matter
- Antiparticles = all of their properties reversed, except mass
- The world's most expensive stuff and a potential superfuel

Did you think I was mere science fiction? Think again! I'm a science fact, baby, and you'd better get used to me! I am matter's evil twin and the nemesis of every atom inside your body. When my dark mirror-image (anti) particles come into contact with particles of matter, we mutually destroy one another in a flash of raw energy.

All of my mass is transferred instantly into superenergetic gamma rays—a return on investment unheard of in the energy generation game—making me around ten billion times more powerful than burning oil. A half gram of me would be enough to set off a Hiroshima-size blast. I am just the ticket to power spacecraft to the stars, but I'm fiendishly hard to produce and, with a track record for the destruction of matter, devilishly tricky to store.

Date of discovery: 1927

- Discoverers: Paul Dirac; CERN (1995)
- Amount made per year: 0.000000005g
- Cost per milligram: $300 billion

Antimatter

CHAPTER 6

Nuclear Heavies

You wouldn't think that these tiny fellows could pack such a punch, but this bunch of heavy hitters can do a lot of damage. Renegades expelled from the wreckage of heavy atoms as their nuclei break apart, the Nuclear Heavies wreak havoc wherever they go. They burn skin, cause cancer, and trigger nuclear bomb blasts—in short, things get nasty fast when these troublemakers show up. But it's mostly thanks to them that we know so much about the weird life of the Atom Family. These quantum thugs truly are to die for!

Radioactivity

Alpha Particle

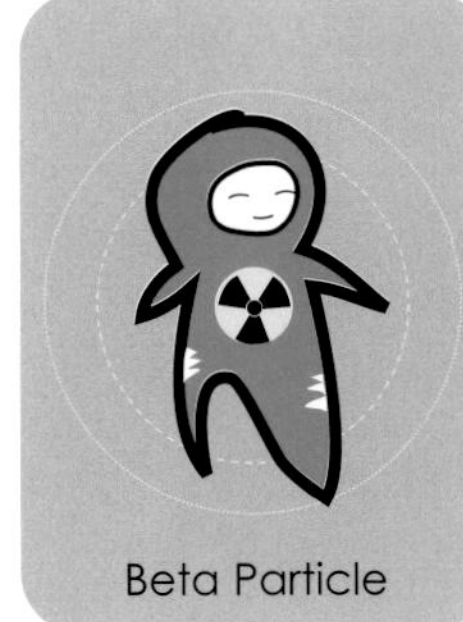
Beta Particle

Photon

Schrödinger's Cat

Weak Force

Radioactivity

Nuclear Heavies

- What happens when atoms break down
- An unpleasant character used to date ancient artifacts
- Detected by a Geiger counter and measured in becquerels

Handle me with care—I'm well known to be touchy and temperamental. Like a sickness, I affect atoms that have more than 83 protons in the nucleus. I am the offspring of a titanic battle between electromagnetism and the strong force, which causes the nuclei of heavy atoms to split apart. This atomic temper tantrum spits out sprays of alpha and beta particles and bursts of gamma rays.

Before I was properly understood, I killed many scientists, but I can be put to good use. I am used in nuclear power plants, and I also sterilize food and kill cancer cells. My level of activity is measured by the length of my "half-life"—the time it takes me to break down half of the atoms in an object. I hang around for ages—this is why toxic nuclear waste oozes into soil and poisons water for years.

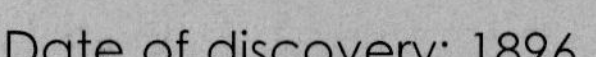

Date of discovery: 1896

- Discoverer: Henri Becquerel
- Half-life of uranium-235: 700 million years
- Worst nuclear accident: Chernobyl (now in Ukraine) (1986)

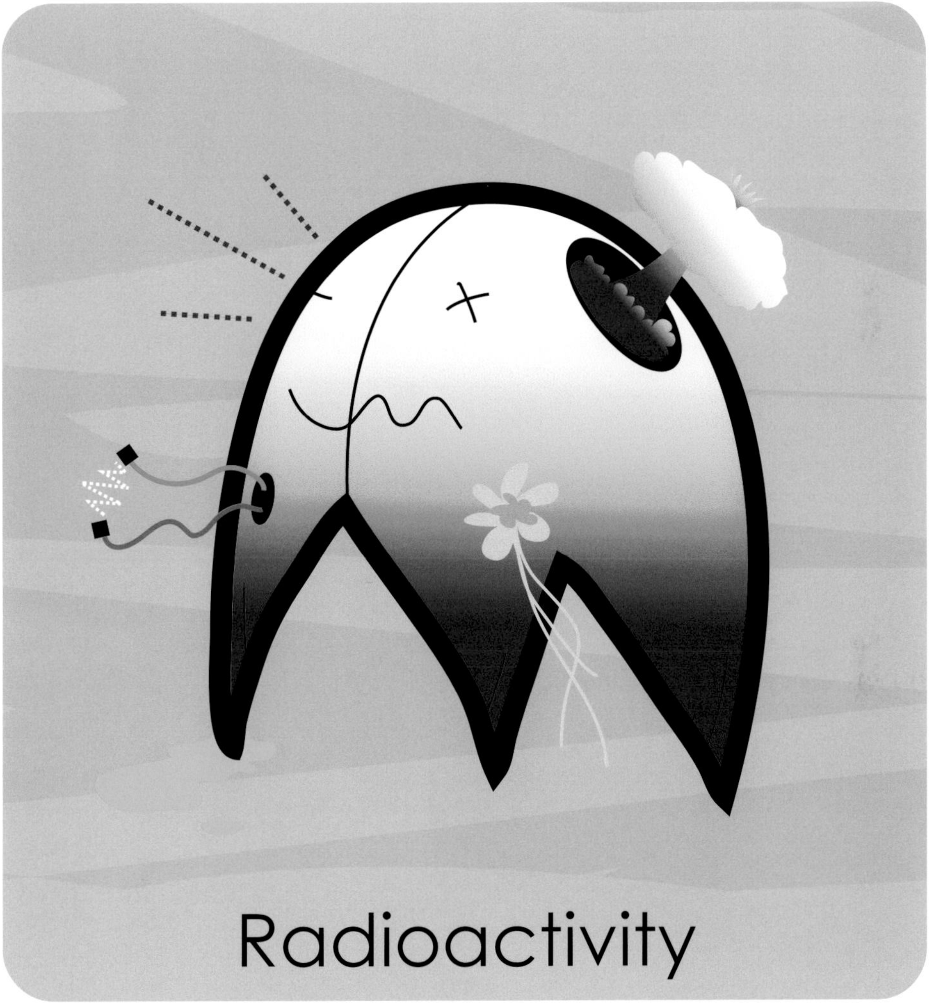

Radioactivity

Alpha Particle

Nuclear Heavies

- The biggest particle of nuclear radiation
- Slow moving, heavy, and very destructive
- Can be stopped by a thin sheet of paper

As far as things go in the teeny-weeny world of subatomic particles, I am a big, ugly bruiser. I'm as chunky as a helium atom's nucleus (in fact, that's what I really am). In short, don't mess with me—better stay clear!

I have a mean streak as wide as the Grand Canyon. When I get inside your body, I plow into atoms, wreaking havoc with your cells and causing cancer. Luckily for you, just a few layers of skin are enough to stop me from getting inside. I was unlucky, however, for Russian journalist Alexander Litvinenko, whom I killed in 2006 after he was fed the alpha-particle-emitting isotope polonium-210.

Smokers, beware—I'm found in cigarettes, but as a vital component of smoke detectors, I could save your life, too.

Date of discovery: 1898

- Discoverer: Ernest Rutherford
- Weight: 6.644656×10^{-27}kg
- Made of two protons and two neutrons

Alpha Particle

Beta Particle

Nuclear Heavies

- This vivacious dude = a fast-moving particle of nuclear radiation
- A negative "free" electron, stopped by a thin sheet of metal
- More than 7,000 times lighter than an alpha particle

I burst out of a decaying radioactive atom's nucleus like a bat out of heck. I've got places to go, and I don't want to hang around! But I need help to escape from an overcrowded nucleus. My good friend Weak Force makes a neutron change into a proton, which creates me in the process, and I'm outta there!

I am so much smaller and lighter than alpha particles that I can zip through materials more easily. This makes me very dangerous for humans. I'll travel right through your skin and can damage the DNA in your body's cells. I'm used for finding leaks in pipes, controlling thickness in paper and sheet-metal production, and sterilizing food. In medicine, I'm used as a "tracer" to track the body's inner workings and make 3-D scans of it.

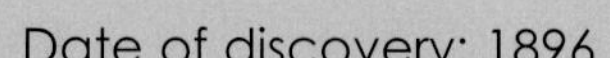

Date of discovery: 1896

- Discoverer: Henri Becquerel
- Mass: 9.109×10^{-31}kg
- Common medical tracer: strontium-90

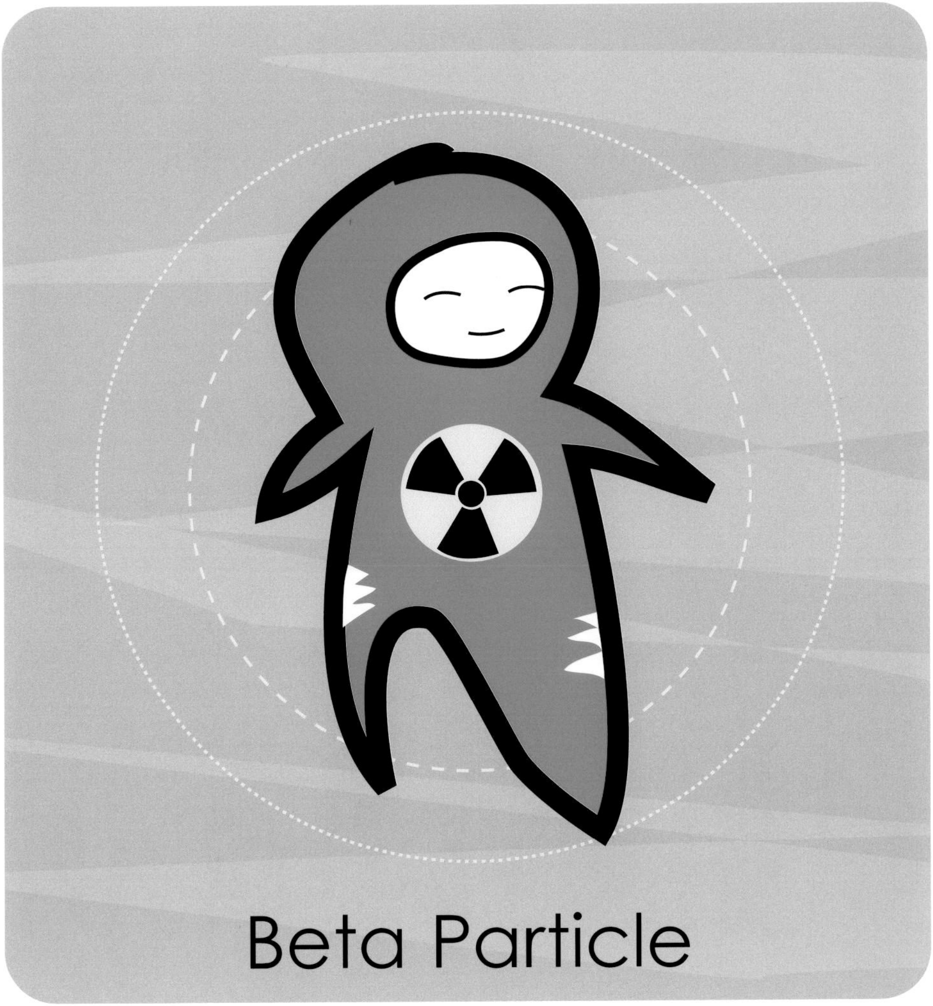

Beta Particle

Photon

Nuclear Heavies

- A real live wire who brings sparkle and fizz wherever he goes
- The Light Crew all made from this little guy
- Spat out of radioactive nuclei as high-energy gamma rays

I am simply the fastest thing in the universe. I have no mass, so I whiz along at the speed of light. I have bamboozled physicists for years with my ability to act like a particle one second and a wave the next.

I'm also the hardest worker in the universe—I speed between the Sun and Earth in continuous streams, bounce off mirrors so that you can see reflections, and then carry the electromagnetic force around. I die when I interact with anything, and I leap into existence when anything gets overexcited. After my job is done, I'm reabsorbed—after all, I'm only a blip of energy. I bring light to the world, but your eyes need to collect around 100 photons to detect it. I expose photographic films, fade your clothes, and also make solar cells work.

Date of discovery: 1905

- Discoverer: Albert Einstein
- Mass: 0kg
- Acts as both a wave and a particle

Photon

Schrödinger's Cat

Nuclear Heavies

- The subject of a famous cat-astrophic thought experiment
- A freaky feline who helps scientists understand the quantum world
- The purr-fect proof that reality is not simple

I was dreamed up by Erwin Schrödinger, and since then I've been living in a box, neither alive nor dead. Let me explain: in the world of subatomic particles, very weird things go on that don't happen in the everyday world. These "quantum" effects make sure that particles have properties, such as speed, only when they are observed. Erwin was trying to figure out what this meant for more fun things such as cats. He asked scientists to imagine me shut inside a box with a radioactive source. If the source decays, it releases poison gas from a bottle and I kick the bucket. If not, I stay alive! But until someone looks inside the box, the source has neither decayed nor *not* decayed—so I am neither alive nor dead!

Date of discovery: 1935

- Chance of alpha decay: 50%
- Deadly gas: hydrocyanic acid
- No one has ever tried this experiment!

Schrödinger's Cat

Weak Force

Nuclear Heavies

- The force of attraction among quarks, electrons, and neutrinos
- A fundamental force that changes the "flavor" of quarks
- Teams up with the strong force in extreme conditions

I have to be honest with you—I'm a little upset to be known as the weak force. I'm no weakling—I'm more than one billion trillion trillion times stronger than gravity! Okay, so I am thousands of times weaker than electromagnetism, but because I battle with feisty protons in the cramped confines of an atom's nucleus, you can hardly call me a wimp!

I work only over tiny distances, but I have bigtime effects. Without my force, the Sun wouldn't shine. At the crucial point in the fusion reaction in the Sun's core, I work my magic on the quarks in a proton, which changes into a neutron. This releases trillions of neutrinos, which pour out of the Sun and stop the reaction from grinding to a halt. I can also change neutrons into protons in unstable atoms, a trick that releases a radioactive beta particle.

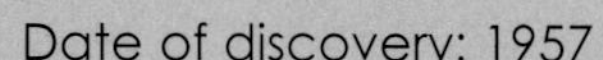
Date of discovery: 1957

- Discoverers: Glashow, Salam, & Weinberg
- Range: around 10^{-18}m
- Carriers: W, W+, and Z particles

Weak Force

CHAPTER 7

Electric Cuties

Danger! High voltage! Don’t be fooled—the Electric Cuties aren’t quite the darling dears that they’d have you believe. Electricity is a form of energy—misuse it and this bunch will punish you hard. Sparks always fly when these twisted devils get together. They are also shockingly hip. The undisputed masters of modernity, they are in charge of running every electronic gadget in the world, as well as generating electricity. The beating heart of this gang and the source of its amazing powers is electromagnetism—a fundamental force of nature.

Static Electricity

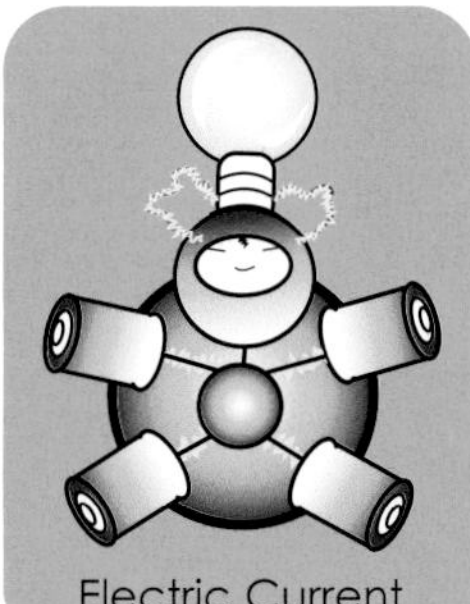
Electric Current

Magnetism

Electromagnetism

Generator

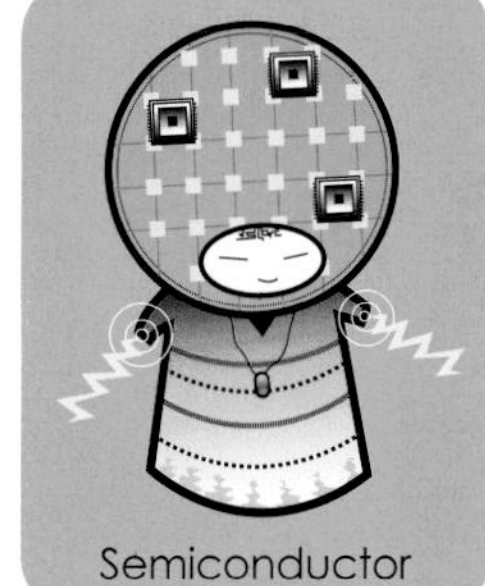
Semiconductor

Static Electricity

Electric Cuties

- Electrical charge that stays in one place
- Hair-raising character who causes lightning
- A bright spark that'll give you a real charge

People say that I'm a useless nuisance. I like to hang around on the surface of things, going nowhere fast. But I'm full of surprises—I provide the crackle when you take off your sweater, and I'll give you a little shock just to remind you that I'm there! I may not be as dynamic as an electric current, but don't think I'm lazy. When I move, I'm gone in a flash. As lightning, I kill around 1,000 people per year.

I'm caused when two electrical insulators rub together. Electrons get scraped off one surface and then put onto the other, leaving each surface with the opposite electrical charge. My irresistible attraction to opposite charges is used in ink-jet printers and photocopiers to pull electrically charged ink onto the paper. I also control the flow of currents in most electronic circuits.

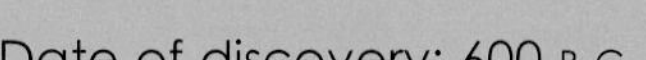

Date of discovery: 600 B.C.

- Typical lightning current: 10,000 amps
- Typical lightning voltage: 100 million volts
- Typical lightning temperature: 30,000°C (54,000°F)

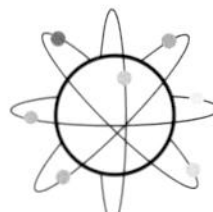

Static Electricity

Electric Current

Electric Cuties

- A form of energy carried by moving electrical charges
- "Jump-started" by a famous frog's-leg experiment
- A shocking phenomenon, measured in amps

I'm nothing like my lazy brother, Static Electricity. My electrons like to go with the flow, and with their help, I light up the world. No question, I'm the man of the past 200 years. Without me, there would be no TV, phones, or computers—life would be pretty dull because there wouldn't even be electric light bulbs!

As a sparky form of energy, I can be turned into light, sound, or motion, but I need a complete circuit in order to work. The chemical potential energy in batteries provides the "push" to move the electrons around. But although I zap around circuits in the blink of an eye, the electrons actually move very slowly. Be careful if I'm around—my jolts jangle up the atoms, cells, and nerves inside your body, giving you a nasty shock. Too much of my power is lethal.

Date of discovery: 1799

- Discoverer: Alessandro Volta
- Speed of electrons in a wire: 0.1mm/s
- Lethal current: 5–8 amps

Electric Current

Magnetism

Electric Cuties

- An invisible force caused only by certain solids and fluids
- Magnets = have north and south poles that attract each other
- Neither of Earth's magnetic poles actually at the geographic pole

I may not be a fundamental force, but I'm not useless. I'm bipolar, with a strong north-south divide. Sprinkle iron filings near me and you'll see that I'm surrounded by an invisible field of force, which gets its power from my atoms. The spin of their electrons makes every one slightly magnetic, but the effect becomes noticeable only when billions of them line up in the same direction.

I'm an integral part of Earth—use me to get your bearings with a compass. I also protect you from deadly cosmic rays. Cassettes and videotapes once used strips of magnetic tape to record information, but now people prefer laser technology. I am found in computer hard drives, ATM cards, and security tags. The magnets in hospital MRI machines can rip a watch off your arm.

Earliest known use: 2 B.C.

- North Pole (estimate): 82.7°N 114.4°W
- South Pole (estimate): 63.5°S 138.0°E

- Shifting of magnetic poles: 40km/year (25 mi./year)

Magnetism

Electromagnetism

Electric Cuties

- Attraction and repulsion between electrically charged objects
- The second-strongest fundamental force, but the most useful
- A helpful fellow carried from place to place by the Light Crew

Forget anything written by those two circus clowns, Weak and Strong Forces! No doubt they've been filling your head with their hot air about how powerful they are. Welcome to the real world! Gravity and I are the only forces that matter outside the ridiculously tiny distances of the atomic nucleus. You actually *feel* us.

I'm the rule that opposites attract. I cause attraction between opposite-charged particles and repulsion between like-charged particles. I keep electrons happy hanging around atoms, get electric currents moving, and allow matter to hold its shape. I stop you from sinking through your chair and your hand from going through this book. I'm the dream-team combo of electric and magnetic fields, and I move around at the speed of light.

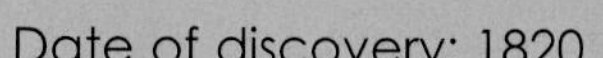

Date of discovery: 1820

- Discoverer: Hans Christian Oersted
- Range: infinite
- Carrier: photon

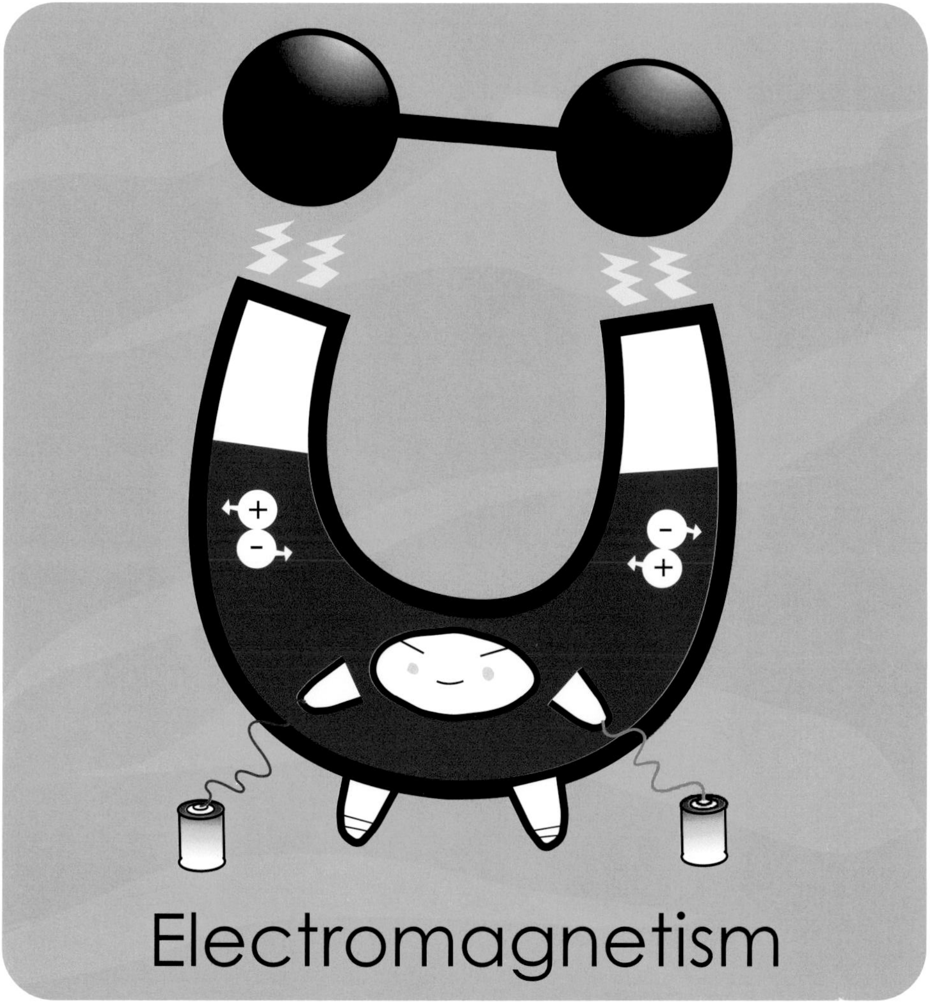

Electromagnetism

Generator

Electric Cuties

- A dynamic dervish who generates electricity
- Uses electromagnetism to supply us with energy
- Powers houses and industry, runs trains, and recharges batteries

Cool, calm, and collected, I'm the backbone of the modern world. Ultimately, all of your energy needs are met by me. Quiet and unassuming, I do my work behind the scenes but with dash and panache, if I may say so.

My flair is for "magicking" electricity out of thin air using electromagnetism. It's simplicity itself. Spin a coil of wire inside a magnetic field and the electrons in the wire get up on their toes and move—you have yourself an electric current. (The generators used in power plants actually spin electromagnets inside huge coils of wire.) The secret of my success is that the fundamental electromagnetic force is made up of magnetic and electric fields. If only one field is there, electromagnetism has the knack of automatically generating the other.

Date of discovery: 1831

- Discoverer: Michael Faraday
- First generator: Hippolyte Pixii (1832)
- Output of largest power plant: 18.2 GW

Generator

Semiconductor

Electric Cuties

- Strange material that doesn't really like to conduct electricity
- Every digital device jam-packed with this clever fellow
- A logical genius and star of the show in computers

I'm a technological wizard. I "conduct" affairs in every piece of electronic equipment, telling electric currents where to go and how to act. The funny thing is, I'm not very good at conducting electricity, but I've made my vice a virtue.

I'm made using chemical elements known as semimetals—strange materials that don't quite know whether they are metals or nonmetals. But I can't perform unless I've had some impurities added first. This "doping" lets electric currents flow, but only in certain directions, which is the key to my fantastic usefulness. When semiconductor "sandwiches" are laid down in microchips, it allows all types of complicated logic decisions and makes me the "brain" of computers.

Date of discovery: 1947

- Discoverer: Bell Laboratories
- Common materials: silicon, germanium
- Industry value: $200 billion per year

Semiconductor

INDEX

GLOSSARY

Antiparticle A subatomic particle with the same mass as a particle of normal matter but with opposite properties. Antimatter is made up of antiparticles.

Baryon A subatomic particle made of three quarks. Protons and neutrons are baryons.

Black hole The densest thing in the universe. So massive that not even light can escape its gravity.

Carrier wave A wave that is modulated, or "tuned," to carry information. FM and AM are ways of modulating radio waves to send information.

Chain reaction A nucleus-splitting atomic reaction that quickly snowballs. Used in nuclear reactors and atom bombs.

Doping Adding impurities to an electrical nonconducting material to make it a semiconductor.

Field of force The area where one object feels a force from another object (e.g., gravitational attraction).

Fission Splitting the nuclei of heavy atoms.

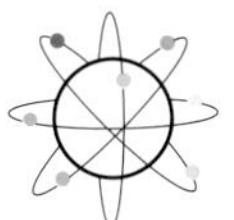

Fundamental force One of four crucial interactions that govern how the universe works. Electromagnetism and gravity are long range; the strong and weak forces are short range.

Fundamental particle The most basic part of matter—a particle that can't be split into smaller, simpler parts.

Fusion Joining together the nuclei of light atoms.

Isotope Atoms of the same element that have the same number of protons but differing amounts of neutrons. Heavy isotopes are often radioactive.

Lepton A small fundamental particle affected by weak forces. Electrons and neutrinos are leptons.

Meson A subatomic particle made of two quarks.

Nucleus The heart of an atom, composed of protons and neutrons.

Quantum theory A strange branch of physics that shows how light can act like a particle and how electrons and other particles have wavelike properties.

GLOSSARY

Radiation sickness Damage to DNA in the cells of the body caused by alpha and beta particles, gamma rays, and neutrons. Can be lethal.

Radioactive dating A way of figuring out the age of rocks, fossils, bones, and other ancient materials by calculating the number of radioactive atoms that have decayed.

Ring of Fire A circle of intense earthquake activity around the edges of the Pacific Ocean, caused by the movement of Earth's tectonic plates.

Sonic boom A "thunderclap" when the shock wave from an airplane breaking the sound barrier—traveling faster than the speed of sound—touches the ground.

Subatomic Anything smaller than an atom.

Thought experiment An imaginary scenario dreamed up by a scientist to test out a theory.

Tracer A radioactive substance that is put inside the body to track the workings of the internal organs.